Chocolate
~ a temptation few can resist.

ETIQUETTE

FOR

CHOCOLATE

LOVERS

Compiled by
Beryl Peters

Copper Beech Publishing

Published in Great Britain by
Copper Beech Publishing Ltd 1997
© Beryl Peters 1997

ISBN 1 898617 17 1

A CIP catalogue record for this book is available from the
British Library.

Editor: Jan Barnes

Copper Beech Gift Books
Copper Beech Publishing Ltd
P O Box 159 East Grinstead
Sussex England RH19 4FS

"Chocolate ... is an invention so noble,
that it should be the nourishment
of the gods, rather than
nectar or ambrosia."

Paris 1684

INTRODUCTION

❧ *Theobroma Cacao - Food of the Gods* ❧

The original name for the chocolate tree means 'Food of the Gods'. There can be no better description than this to evoke the mystic and romantic history of chocolate which is as diverse as myths, legends and court intrigues to piracy and smuggling.

Starting from humble beginnings as a cocoa drink prepared by Central American natives in the 15th century, its position was elevated to that of a status symbol as it was sipped by the rich and powerful in the fashionable 17th century chocolate houses. Only later was it made for eating.

So the adventurous tale of chocolate passed through the 19th and 20th centuries, developing from a frothy thick drink to today's mouth watering confections, tempting the taste buds with its many textures and flavours.

The temptation of chocolate is here to stay; whether eaten in abundance or nibbled as a special treat. For me though, it will always represent a token of love and for this reason I would like to dedicate this book to my husband Graham, a true chocolate lover.

Beryl Peters

THEOBROMA CACAO - FOOD OF THE GODS

THE COCOA TREE

The original name for the chocolate tree, 'Theobroma Cacao' translates as 'Food of the Gods'. The tree grows in the fertile soil of the tropical belt between the tropics of Cancer and Capricorn.

The evergreen tree grows 15-25 feet tall, with dark green leaves about 8 inches long. A tree will bear over 6,000 flowers in one year, but no more than 60 will mature into fruit.

The cocoa flowers are small, frail and scentless, growing in tufts and clusters with five yellow petals on a rose coloured calyx.

The mature fruit is a pulpy pod weighing 10-20 ounces. When ripe, it is golden yellow or crimson tinged with purple.

THEOBROMA CACAO - FOOD OF THE GODS

CACAO.COCOA.CHOCOLATL.CHOCOLATE

THE COCOA NAME

The Aztecs called the cocoa tree 'cocauatl' and named their frothy drink derived from it, 'chocolatl'.

How it came to be known as chocolate, depends on who you listen to – but Thomas Gage's 1648 survey says that the name is compounded from '*atte*', a Mexican word meaning water, and '*choco*' which was the sound made when cocoa and water were mixed together in a cup.

It is speculated that 'cocoa' originated from either bad spelling of cacao, or coconut which Dr Johnson spelt as 'cocoanut'!

CACAO.COCOA.CHOCOLATL.CHOCOLATE

COMPLETE CHOCOLATIERE.

CHOCOLATE
TO DRINK

"Chocolate is not only pleasant to taste,
but it is a veritable balm for the mouth,
for the maintaining of all glands
in a good state of health;
thus it is that all who drink it
possess a sweet breath."

Blancardi 1705

LEGENDS, GODS AND EMPERORS

Aztec legend tells of cocoa being consumed by the gods in paradise.

The ancient Aztecs of Mexico and the Incas of Peru were probably the first people to use cocoa as food.

Cortes mistaken for the 'God of the Air' ...

The Aztecs were waiting for their 'God of the Air' Quatzalcoatl to return from exile. When the Spanish adventurer Hernando Cortes reached their shore, fair-skinned and bearded like their God, he was welcomed to the land and served his first drink of chocolate.

❧

✐ frothy drink ...

At this stage in its history, the drink was being made from cocoa, cinnamon, aniseed and cornmeal.

The cocoa beans were roasted, shelled and ground, then moulded into cakes. These cakes were used when required by mixing them with water and whisked with an instrument called a molinet to make the frothy drink.

It was Cortes who realised the commercial importance of the strange beans before anyone else. When Cortes conquered Mexico in 1519 he captured the Aztec chieftain-styled Emperor, Montezuma.

❧

Golden goblets ...

Montezuma loved the spiced chocolate and drank it from golden or painted gourd goblets every day.

According to written evidence,
Montezuma always drank a full goblet
of chocolate prior to entering his harem!

CHOCOLATE ETIQUETTE

As early as the 16th century, some important etiquette notes were found:

'And then they ended with the chocolate ... to carry it one placed the cup in his right hand. He did not go taking it by its rims but likewise went placing the gourd in the palm of his hand ... But those who followed, all were served with only earthen cups.

This glimpse of chocolate etiquette ... tells us that the fine gourd and calabash cups were for the higher echelons while lesser mortals drank theirs from clay cups.' ⋆

⋆ © **The True History of Chocolate**
by **Sophie and Michael Coe. See acknowledgements.**

⋆⇒◉⇐⋆

CHOCOLATE REACHES SPAIN

Cortes discovered how the drink was made
and cocoa beans were then regularly sent
from Mexico to Spain for the making of
chocolate.

The Spanish added sugar ...
When King Ferdinand and Queen Isabella
of Spain were first presented with this drink
they didn't like it.

Sugar was added and mixed with other
flavourings such as cinnamon, nutmeg, cloves,
mint, oranges and vanilla to make the drink
more palatable. They loved these new vari-
ations and tried to keep them a secret for
almost a century!

✥

Galleons carried gold and cocoa ...

The Spaniards rated gold as a most important product, but also greatly valued cocoa beans. Many of the galleons which sailed between Spain and the New World carried gold and cocoa.

Sometimes the English captured the galleons and at that time English sailors used to throw the cocoa beans overboard as rubbish, after tasting their bitter flavour!

It is said of Queen Maria Theresa, the wife of King Louis XIV of France, that she only had two passions – the King and chocolate!

1660

17

⤖⚬⟞⟝

THE SECRET OF CHOCOLATE
REACHES ENGLAND

Monks took the secret to France and Germany and from there, chocolate was brought to England. Records show that the new chocolate drink was taken frequently at Oxford as early as 1650.

✒

*H*ot and sweet for fashionable London ...

The original coarse Mexican beverage, containing no sugar and flavoured with spices, was served as cool. This was not acceptable in fashionable London; the drink had to be hot and sweet to make it palatable to European tastes.

CHOCOLATE ETIQUETTE

The dutiful servant will discreetly
indicate to a gentleman guest should
any froth or cream from the cocoa drink
attach itself to his moustache or beard.

CHOCOLATE ETIQUETTE

Servants should remember that if the cocoa
pot has been standing or simmering long
on the fire, evaporation will have occurred
so more hot water should be added and the
contents of the pot should be well stirred
with a glass rod before serving.

Elegant and refined people ...

At the same time as the frequenting of coffee houses was passing from the fashionable to the populace, elegant and refined people began to gather at the chocolate houses.

After the restoration in 1660, the price of chocolate was about 10 to 15 shillings a pound – so this new but costly drink was all the more alluring to the privileged (wealthy) few!

Chocolate was a luxury ...

Although the cocoa bean arrived in Europe a century before the tea leaf or the coffee berry it took decades to establish itself in the home.

Tea and coffee were easy to prepare, but cocoa was more difficult and expensive, so there is little wonder that cocoa advanced very slowly as an everyday drink! Indeed, chocolate was a luxury rather than a necessity.

∾

Servants prepare the drink ...

The process of making a chocolate drink was lengthy, complicated and costly, but sometimes the rich bought chocolate so that their servants could prepare the drink at home.

The solid chocolate cake had to be sliced very finely into a jug. A small amount of sugar was then added, followed by a little boiling water. This was gradually worked up into a smooth paste and the cup then filled with hot water and milk. This drink would then be whisked to a froth and served from a chocolate jug.

CHOCOLATE ETIQUETTE

When the young gentleman returns
to the house after depleting the body
by taking physical exercise,
the dutiful servant will allow time
for the young gentleman
to perform his ablutions and cool down
before presenting him
with his nourishing cup of hot chocolate.

❦

Soluble Cocoa ...

In the 1830s, many people experimented to make a powdered cocoa that would be less fatty and more easy to use.

Van Houten, a Dutch chemist developed a hydraulic press that could leave the cocoa ready for pulverising. He then 'Dutched' it with potassium or sodium carbonates. Cocoa then required the simple addition of boiling water to prepare it for the table and it could be placed on an equal footing with tea and coffee.

❦

Now available to the poor ...

When cocoa could thus be prepared a new era began for its use. Now it needed neither apparatus nor time and was more readily prepared than either tea or coffee. As a result, it became available to the poor for whom it was like a food.

Smuggling ...

High taxation on cocoa beans in the 18th century made the smuggling of them worthwhile along with brandy and tobacco. Around Bristol in England there was much smuggling:

"*...the smuggled chocolate was daily hawked around the streets of Bristol, Bath, Salisbury, Worcester and Birmingham*" 1776

Before 1820, the duty levied on chocolate was one shilling and sixpence per pound and every pound of chocolate had to be wrapped in papers supplied by revenue officers!

THE CHOCOLATE HOUSES OF LONDON TOWN

The first 'chocolate house' was opened by a Frenchman in King's Head Alley, Bishopsgate Street in 1657. For over a hundred years the price of chocolate remained very high but still the chocolate houses did a good trade.

Famous clubs ...

Many of the chocolate houses later became famous as clubs. They became political meeting places and the proprietors had to make sure that the opposite sides didn't meet! The Cocoa Tree and Ozinda's became the favourite place for high Tories whilst the leading Whigs would go to St James's Coffee House.

✌ফ
✌A Royal Decree ...

In 1675 King Charles II made a Royal Decree to suppress chocolate houses because they had become gambling houses!

As a result, by 1702 only five chocolate houses remained:

The Chocolate House at Blackheath;

The Cocoa Tree, Pall Mall;

Lindhearts, King Street Bloomsbury;

The Spreadeagle, Covent Garden - and Whites, St James Street.

Chocolate was still served in some coffee houses and cost one shilling a quart, or two pence a dish – double the price of tea or coffee!

CHOCOLATE RECIPES

For a Chocolate Drink ~ 1672

Some of the best chocolate is made in this manner:- take a ball of chocolate which is made only of cocoa and "Notty" which is the fruit of a tree. It is much of the nature of saffron, is cordial, of a pleasant colour and is dearer than silver!

The Method

Grate it into a ship bisket, finely beaten or grated: then take half milk or water; make it boil and when it boileth put in your bread and chocolate together and let it boil a little more; sweeten it with sugar and sup it very hot, without frothing.

If you please you may froth it in your chocolate pot with a molinet.

CHOCOLATE RECIPES

The Way To Make Very Nice Chocolate

Take one square of chocolate (vanilla) for each person and half a pint of milk; grate the chocolate into a very fine powder, put it into the milk when quite boiling, let it boil twenty minutes, stirring it all the time, and serve it up fresh from the fire.

Conan Doyle's famous detective character, Sherlock Holmes, drank cocoa at breakfast.

ROYAL CHOCOLATE LOVERS

Inventories for the Royal collections show a large number of items used for chocolate drinking, including:

'Six fine white ribbed Chocolate Cupps'
at Kensington Palace – and silver chocolate pots;

'for one new large Chocolate Pott with a wooden handle.' 1691

ROYAL CHOCOLATE LOVERS

In Hampton Court Palace, England, a 'Chocolate Kitchen' was established as early as 1699:

The 'King's Chocolate Kitchen' which was in the south east angle of the Palace, had windows abutting a little court known as the 'Chocolate Court'.

The appearance of the chocolate kitchen may have been similar to the Confectionery which was being set up in the Palace at the same time – for the indulgence of the Royal sweet tooth.

"Warmed chocolate paste
can be applied externally to cure all kinds of
inflammation ... it is a cooler, doth assuage all
pains and mitigates the pain of gout and
old age pains." 1672

CHOCOLATE
TO EAT

Ladies – Don't Put Chocolate
In Your Drawers!

**Chocolate readily takes up odours:
Sometimes ladies utterly spoil the taste
of the content of a gift box of chocolates
by putting it in a clothes drawer which
contains moth balls.**

CHOCOLATE TO EAT

Cakes of chocolate in the 17th century contained a small proportion of cocoa nib with sugar and spices; it remained coarse until Van Houten invented the cocoa press.

*C*hocolate as a medicine ...

Sir Hans Sloane was physician to Samuel Pepys and in 1727 was the first surgeon to King George II. He valued chocolate highly as a restorative and was credited with being the first person to produce a solid confection combining milk and chocolate.

This preparation was expensive and regarded as having great value as a medicine.

Sold Here
Sir Hans Sloane's
Milk Chocolate

Made (only) by William White, *Succefsor to* M.ʳ Nicholas Sanders, N.ᵒ 8 *Greek Street, Soho,* London.

Greatly recommended by feveral eminent Physicians efpecially those of *Sir Hans Sloane's* Acquaintance. For its Lightnefs on the Stomach, & its great Ufe in all Confumptive Cases.

N.B. What is not figned with my Name and fealed with my Arms, is Counterfeit.

Reproduced by courtesy of Messrs. Cadbury Bros., Ltd.

⊷━◎━⊷

THE CHOCOLATE MAKERS

In 1795, Dr Joseph Fry of Bristol first used a
steam engine to drive chocolate machines and
the price of chocolate making began to fall.

✍

*Q*uakers become chocolate makers...

The Society of Friends (Quakers) was founded
in England to promote justice, equality and
understanding. Quakers were barred from
many traditional professions, so turned to
chocolate to make their living.

Fry's, Rowntree's, Cadbury's and other
firms started manufacturing cocoa and chocolate.

The Quakers developed some of the best
working conditions for their workers, spon-
soring housing, health schemes and education.

CHOCOLATE ETIQUETTE

On nanny's day off, a dutiful servant
will remember that a fretful
infant can be calmed considerably
by a drink of sweet, warm chocolate
without having to disturb the mistress.

CHOCOLATE ETIQUETTE

When the maid sees that the evening is
drawing prematurely to a close because of
lack of enthusiasm, she would do well to
suggest to madame that she revive the
company by offering them a selection
of eating chocolates.

The famous Hershey Bar

In the early 19th century, large numbers of Quakers went to Pennsylvania, USA and by 1864 Milton Hershey, also a Quaker, had set up his sweet factory.

In 1892, Hershey decided to sell his caramel factory and change to chocolate making and he soon set up a model village similar to those in England. Hershey's village was to become known as 'Hershey, The Chocolate Town'.

After experimentation he discovered that by using solid vegetable fats instead of cocoa butter, the chocolate bar wouldn't melt in hot weather.

The modern American Hershey Bar was waiting to be invented!

-+=◉=+-

CHOCOLATE AND THE TRAVELLER

Pure cocoa is to travellers, cyclists and all who are subject to exposure, a beverage of unquestionable value.

In travelling, the chocolate sticks are a most convenient refreshment, containing in a very small compass a large amount of nutritious matter. They serve to protect the stomach from the injurious effects of the long-continued abstinence; a small cake being amply sufficient for a day.

CHOCOLATES IN FANCY BOXES.

				Price to retailer.	Price to wholesale houses.
				per gro.	per gro.
½d.	Boxes	Crêmes, gross and ½-gross boxes	...	4/3	4/-
1d.	do.	Crêmes, ½-gross boxes, square ...	...	8/8	8/1
1d.	do.	Chocolate do. (new) ...	...	8/9	8/3
				per doz.	per doz.
1/-	do.	Crêmes, containing 12 1d. boxes ...	...	8/9	8/3
1/-	do.	Chocolate do. do.	...	9/-	8/9
				per gro.	per gro.
2d.	do.	Mexican Chocolate ¼-gross boxes	...	17/-	15/6
				per doz.	per doz.
3d.	do.	Crêmes ... 2-doz. boxes	...	2/4	2/2
3d.	do.	Dragées ... 2-doz. do.	...	2/4	2/2
4d.	do.	Crêmes ... 1-doz. do.	...	3/1	2/10
6d.	do.	Fancy Foil, containing 12 ½d. sticks	...	4/6	4/3
6d.	Cleopatra Needles, ½ doz. in box	..	...		
6d.	Boxes	Charcoal Crêmes, containing 6 1d. Tablets			
6d.	do.	Vanilla, containing 12 ½d. sticks	...		
6d.	do.	Crêmes, Dragées, or Pralines, slide, oval, square, or new square			
6d.	do.	Fruit Delices			
6d.	do.	Crêmes or Pralines, oval or square ...			
1/-	do.	Vanilla Chocolate, containing 24 ½d. sticks			
1/-	do.	Fruit Delices, new patterns		4/3	4/-
1/-	do.	Best Crêmes ... (round)			
1/-	do.	Dessert Chocolate { white } Parisian		8/6	7/9
1/-	do.	Crêmes Pralines (boxes)			
1/-	do.	containing 2 doz. ½d. Crême Shells ...			
1/-	do.	Bonbons (Plain), new oval box ...			
1/6	do.	Square, with Pictures		13/-	12/3
2/-	do.	Olive-wood boxes		17/6	16/-
2/6	do.	Round boxes		22/6	21/-
2/6	do.	Pictures on top (new)		21/6	20/-
3/-	do.	Satin (new)		30/-	28/-
5/-	do.	Caskets (new)		48/-	48/-
5/-	do.	Casket (hexagon shape) new and choice		48/-	48/-

CROQUETTES.

1/-	do.	in upright round boxes, 20 pastilles	...	8/6	7/9
6d.	do.	do. 20 do.	...	4/3	4/-
3d.	do.	do. ½-gross boxes	...	2/4	2/2

CHOCOLATE PARTY ETIQUETTE

Chocolate Easter Eggs were available from the mid 19th century, changing the traditional 'Egg Parties' at Easter into a delicious treat.

When Easter Egg parties are given for children they should arrive about three o'clock and hunt for Easter Eggs which are hidden in the house or garden. These eggs should be a mixture of cardboard ones filled with chocolates and painted hard-boiled eggs. After serving a light tea, the party should come to an end by six o'clock. This is quite late enough for young children!

CHOCOLATE RECIPES

Chocolate Biscuits

3oz flour	1oz cocoa butter
3oz ground cocoa	1 beaten egg
2oz sugar	1 tbsp milk
½ tsp vanilla	pinch of salt

Mix the cocoa and sugar together, add the melted cocoa butter in a saucepan and stir over a low heat until the mixture is melted. Add the vanilla and gradually work in the flour and salt, then add the milk and finally the egg. Keep the mixture warm, roll out on a floured board and cut the rounds. Bake in a moderate oven for 5 - 10 mins.

The biscuits may be dredged with fine sugar or they may be coated with melted chocolate.

CHOCOLATE RECIPES

Chocolate Meringue Pie

Mix half a cupful of cocoa with a quarter of a cupful of cornflour, half a cupful of sugar, a quarter of a teaspoonful of salt, three yolks of eggs, and a pint of milk.

Cook over hot water until thick, stirring constantly. Flavour with one teaspoonful of vanilla extract and pour into a baked pie crust shell. Beat up the whites of the eggs to a stiff froth, add three tablespoonfuls of sugar, and beat again. Place this meringue on the top of the pie, brown lightly in the oven and serve cold.

CHOCOLATE RECIPES

Tempting Chocolate Cake

Beat together two-thirds of a cupful of butter and one cupful of sugar, add three eggs well beaten, one cupful of milk, two and a half cupfuls of flour sifted with two teaspoonfuls of baking-powder and a quarter of a cupful of cocoa, and add one cupful of chopped nuts. Bake in a moderate oven.

CHOCOLATE RECIPES

A Delicious Chocolate Cream

Make a pint of chocolate, with spring water, let it be cold, beat the yolks of 3 eggs, mix it with the chocolate, sweeten it with double refined sugar, strain it, set it on a gentle fire, keep it stirring till it begins to thicken, then pour into your glasses.

**In 1853 Gladstone fixed the duty on
cocoa beans as 1d a pound -
it stayed that way for 60 years.**

⊷⭤◉⭤⊷

ADVERTISING THE DELIGHTS OF COCOA

Cocoa and chocolate advertising was at its height between 1880 and 1914. The following extravagant claims were made:

Pure cocoa is a beverage which, in a very marked manner, reduces the craving for alcoholic stimulants.

Pure cocoa is at once pleasant, brightening and easily digested.

Pure cocoa is a nerve food, a sedative and promotes restfulness and sleep.

ADVERTISING THE DELIGHTS OF COCOA

Pure cocoa is to business men a food
beverage which carries them safely in the
midst of arduous occupation and worry.

Pure cocoa is fit for youth, for middle age,
and for old age – giving 'staying power'
under strain of work, mental and physical.

Pure cocoa is fit for judicious use in the
food of children and invalids.

Pure cocoa is a muscle food.

⁂

ADVERTISING THE DELIGHTS OF COCOA

The London Bus Scheme

On December 3rd 1897, each lady riding on a Road Car Bus or Balls Bros' Bus was given a sample tin of cocoa. The buses were decorated with flags, cocoa pods etc. and the samples were given out by the conductors. 200,000 samples were distributed.

The Daily Telegraph Scheme

Buyers of The Daily Telegraph on September 24th, 1897 would, on showing it to any one of the grocers given in the list printed in The Daily Telegraph, receive a sample of cocoa and a penny stamp to pay for the newspaper.

"At Christmastide chocolate boxes and creams are in universal request."

The Housewife magazine December 1889

CHOCOLATE ETIQUETTE

The Nursery Maid must keep an
observant eye on the children when
eating chocolates are presented to
company. The children must be refrained
from grabbing greedily, offering the choice
to adults first.

Hush, baby, my dolly,
　　I pray you don't cry;
You'll have some Queen Chocolate,
　　With milk, by-and-bye.
Or, do you like Cocoa?
　　If so, have "Elect,"
For to either you're welcome,
　　Which do you select?

⊷≡⊙⊜≺⊷

COCOA AS MONEY

Cocoa beans were so precious that they were used as money in Central America; a rabbit could be purchased for 10 beans and a slave for 100 and the different provinces paid their tribute to the chief in cocoa.

In 1586 Thomas Cavendish stated that 150 beans were exchangeable for a 'Real of Plate'.

"The Indians use no gold or silver to trafficke in or buy withall and unto this day the custom continues as in the province of Mexico, instede of money they use cacao." Joseph Acosta 1604.

Servants like to eat a cocoa porridge for
breakfast.   It is made from lumps of hard
cocoa which is grated and mixed with fine
breadcrumbs, sugar and water or milk.
It gives them energy for their work.

Chocolate Chatter!

The squirrel is a nuisance in cocoa plantations. He's a "wanton waster of cocoa. He gnaws a hole in the pods to get to the sweet pulp and scatters the beans on the ground."

Samuel Pepys in 1661 entered into his diary that he drank chocolate to get rid of his hangover from the festivities surrounding the coronation of Charles II.

Side products from cocoa butter:
Cooking fat; lighting oil (cocoa butter burns in an open clay lamp with a bright flame which neither smokes nor smells); ointments; soft soap; candle fat; fuel; fertiliser.

A lady's diary entry for March 11th 1712 reads "Wednesday, from 8-10, drank two dishes of chocolate in bed and fell asleep after them."

⟶⟹◯⟸⟵

LOVE TOKENS

Chocolate has been used as a gift since the early days. European travellers used to take chocolate for themselves and their hosts.

In the days of chaperoning throughout courtship, one of the early boxes of chocolates was often presented to the young lady by her beau.

In England in the early 20th century, the first Valentine's Day candy box was introduced for sale. This was soon followed in 1922 by the famous Perugina Baci ("Kisses").

The "Kisses" boxed chocolates celebrated romantic love - and now chocolate is still thought of as a love token.

ACKNOWLEDGEMENTS

Thanks to the following companies for their
assistance in compiling this book:

Cadbury Ltd
Nestlé UK Ltd
Cover picture reproduced by kind permission of
Caley's of Norwich Ltd
Chocolate was originally made in the Caley name in
Norwich, England in 1886. Now, over 100 years
later, this name, from Victorian times, can be found
on chocolate again.

Early etiquette notes on page 15 are taken with
permission from
The True History of Chocolate
by Sophie and Michael Coe
Published by Thames & Hudson 1997

Special thanks to Hampton Court Palace.
References and pictures taken from
The History of Hampton Court Palace
by Ernest Law - 1891.

THE ETIQUETTE COLLECTION
Collect the set!

THE ETIQUETTE OF NAMING THE BABY
Traditional names for your baby, their origins and meanings - and the people in history who have shared the names.

THE ETIQUETTE OF AN ENGLISH TEA
How to serve a perfect English afternoon tea; tea traditions, superstitions, recipes.

ETIQUETTE FOR COFFEE LOVERS
Coffee as it ought to be! Friends gathered over a steaming cup of coffee, or those indulging in a single cup will enjoy the story of coffee drinking, recipes and coffee chat.

THE ETIQUETTE OF ENGLISH PUDDINGS
Are you missing a good old-fashioned pudding? English puddings - the traditional way. Delicious recipes which have been used for over 100 years.

A Copper Beech Book makes the perfect gift.
See also our books about parlour games, servants, graphology and social secrets.

Acknowledgements

Thanks to the following companies for their assistance in compiling this book:

Cadbury Ltd
Nestlé UK Ltd
Cover picture reproduced by kind permission of Caley's of Norwich Ltd
Chocolate was originally made in the Caley name in Norwich, England in 1886. Now, over 100 years later, this name, from Victorian times, can be found on chocolate again.

Early etiquette notes on page 15 are taken with permission from
The True History of Chocolate
by Sophie and Michael Coe
Published by Thames & Hudson 1997

Special thanks to Hampton Court Palace.
References and pictures taken from
The History of Hampton Court Palace
by Ernest Law - 1891.

THE ETIQUETTE COLLECTION
Collect the set!

THE ETIQUETTE OF MOTORING
Manners and driving hints for motorists.
Introduction by Lord Montagu of Beaulieu.

THE ETIQUETTE OF LOVE & COURTSHIP
A guide for romantics. Flirting, temptation, first
impressions: essential advice for lovers.

THE ETIQUETTE OF DRESS
Fashion tips from days gone by.

ETIQUETTE FOR GENTLEMEN
No real gentleman should be without these rules for
correct conduct.

For your free catalogue containing details of these and
other Copper Beech Gift Books, write to:

Copper Beech Publishing Ltd
P O Box 159 East Grinstead Sussex England RH19 4FS